A Beating of Wings

Poems by Gertrude Rubin

Cover artist, Leslie Hirshfield
photographer, Bonnie Baron
lay-out editor, Wayne Spelius
editor-at-large, Carol Spelius

LAKE SHORE PUBLISHING

373 Ramsay Road

Deerfield, Illinois

60015

Copyright 1991
ISBN # 0-941363-09-0

$8.95

Dedicated to Philip

and our children,
Michael, Bonnie and Laurie

Special thanks to my distinguished mentors:

Daryl Hine

Ralph J. Mills, Jr.
John F. Nims, Michael Anania
Paul Carroll, founder,
The Writers Program,
University of Illinois at Chicago

Allan Bates
and the late Ted Berrigan,
Northeastern Illinois University

Poets Club of Chicago,
a circle of my peers,
whose critical encouragement
has inspired and informed
my poetry

and to my patient editors
Wayne and Carol Spelius
of LAKE SHORE PUBLISHING

Gertrude Rubin's poems rise from the occasions of her life, from her acute perceivings, with apparent effortlessness, so unobstrusively convincing and natural is her imagination, so developed are her artistic skills. She is an observer of the mundane, the near-at-hand, the ordinary lives and deaths of people, animals, trees and flowers about her -- in short, the range of experiences we all know but seldom penetrate imaginatively. Gertrude Rubin has, over the years, built up a body of poetry that opens the secrets of those experiences. Her work contains the kind of "new" William Carlos Williams said we famish for the lack of. Read these poems -- You will read them again.

Professor Ralph J. Mills, Jr.
English Department,
University of Illinois at Chicago

Herod:
"I tell you there is a wind that blows. And I hear in the air something that is like the beating of wings, like the beating of vast wings. Do you not hear it?"
...from SALOME, Oscar Wilde

Table of Contents

I Vivaldi's Seasons

II Taken From Life

III A Beating of Wings

I

VIVALDI'S SEASONS

A.M. SCENARIO

It begins with a jet plane's
roar. Houses line up
in tight-lipped silence.
Dreamers stir uneasily,
like flotsam swept ashore.
Thunder. Distant timpani.

From fog, trees emerge.
They stiffen, if disaster --
fire, plunder, flood --
hits our block. Or, the TIMES,
flung from a newsboy's wagon
narrowly misses the porch.

Churning trucks. Bravura whistles.
Garbagemen alight, and
lift the cans like props.
Next comes the early jogger,
careful not to look back
at the thing pursuing him.

Now the stage is set:
alarms rung, "curtains up",
and morning greets us,
blushing on cue. Heralded
by a cacophony of lawn mowers,
cab horns, and birdsong.

ESCAPE ARTIST

Will the first narcissus,
slender in a Delft bowl,
bloom forever? Nonsense, --
a paper-white lie. False
as a rose tagged, ETERNAL.

The first day of summer leads
to the first day of winter.
Winter leads to, leads to --
When did the cycle become
another tiresome cliche?

When I crave crawl space
away from Time's whirring,
I slip through a crack
(careful to smooth the crease
so it doesn't show!), and fly

to *Svea's* cafe on Clark St.
Waitresses in tight uniforms
mother the working classes.
King Carl XVI Gustav and
tiaraed Queen Sylvia, smile

from troll-lined walls.
A neighborhood patron, bald
as the titan, Jean Sibelius,
devours Swedish pancakes
with lingonberries. One table

behind, a volume of verse
to savor, I read, read,
for a lifetime. Footsteps,
laughter, clatter of dishes --
sensed, but quickly forgotten.

CASUALTY LIST

The elm is gone.
It was trapped, lassoed
like a dumb animal, and
felled by an ordinary buzz-saw.
Ancient time-rings were stripped
naked, discarded on the curb.
All that remains is the sky behind it.

I sleep in a room, in a house,
younger than those trees.
Last night, when the elm held up
severed wrists to ease the pain,
and let the blood run down, I woke
and heard the roots stir uneasily.

I kept silence, mindful of
my bad habit of saying too much
or too little -- dreading
the elm's last hours.
Rooted near the window,
I wept, helpless as a tree.

NIGHT OF THE DRUIDS

Who picked the last rose,
and pricked Beauty's finger
twice? Why were the birds
suspended in midflight, the
barking dogs struck dumb?
The West wind declining
to answer, draws its breath
like a cello's dark note.

Once,
while alone in the yard,
someone felt closely
watched. Or overlooked.
And, for reasons unknown,
knew the difference, but
not the words to say it.

LATE-BLOOMER

Horse-chestnut buds
paw the air. Earth's
dry mouth cracks open
in neat, pearly rows.
But the woman next door
still hibernates.

She waits until dusk
to fashion her moves.
Cautious as a chess-
player, she advances
a hoard of words, her
carved ivory pawns.

Midnight: the usual
stalemate. She goes out,
scanning the heavens
for images. Big Dipper
is back, cartwheeling
like a homesick tumbler.

The simile reminds her
of one she discarded.
Rueful, she combs the
trash-can like a bear,
foraging scraps: like a
woman hungry for spring.

HOME FREE

The crocus take
three quick nibbles
of snow

and sidelong
glances at the
deserted house.

Any survivors,
this time?
Wait,

someone yanked
up a shade,
windows blink

open like
eyes. Sunlight
fires the bricks.

Everywhere,
a loosening of
pulses. It's

all right,
you can come
out now.

INSIGHT

"IT IS SPRING AND I AM BLIND"
thus read the beggar's sign.
But who, among the sighted,
  glancing up, saw the once
barren trees turn fuzzy green?
  Or knew precisely when
each upside-down, newborn leaf
  was slapped alive, and while
still wobbly on stem, left to
  flourish or die? And who,
hearing a small commotion,
  saw the leaves sprung open,
like tiny accordians?

In his bones, the beggar knew
  it was spring. But who saw
a tell-tale sign: the sight of
  the old magnolia tree
rekindling its tapers, its
  buds shaped like votive lights
on a backyard's forked altar.
  And who saw the buds wake
from an eternity's sleep,
  their petals, too quickly
unfastened and scattered like
  pink-throated prophecies,
fulfilling some grand design?

And if, by chance, these petals
  (the precursors to leaves)
lay like cast-off children, near
  the parent tree-- who, in

quiet reflection, saw the
  petals billowing like
magic carpets, parachutes,
  glider sails; or flocks of
flying frisbees, lightly tossed
  and grounded. The beggar
smiled secretly. Did he "see"
  the splendor that often
escapes our myopic eyes?

END OF SEASON

The planet leans
to one side
like a phantom-ship,
listing. Pumpkins sag,
a peach is overripe,
my hand swells
the apple's curve.

Dry leaves collect
in unlit pyres.
I kick them--
impatient for the
smell of a bonafide
bonfire, the
charcoal taste
of autumns, past.

Clocks turn
back, curtains hang
limp. Gauze sails,
without breeze.
All this silence
thickens my blood,
makes me want
to shout, awaken
summer ghosts, and
act perverse.

Perverse as
the Hunter's Moon
when it sulks
on its red haunches
instead of rising
as expected,
brilliantly.

ENCORE PERFORMANCE

Autumn arrives with operatic flair.
Pompous as tenors, the emblazoned trees
demand center stage. Crimson-caped maples,
leaves showy with arias, regale us
while prima donna willows drag their robes
along the marigold-dotted footlights.
Voices hushed, we gaze up at oaks soaring
like gilt archways of "Tosca's" cathedral.

Yet, weeks later, when the eloquent elms
are shorn, their foliage snatched by the wind
the way Valkyries reclaim dead men's souls,
are we not grateful for a small reprise --
the fallen leaves we found and carrried home,
placing each shape, delicate as brush-stroke,
on white tablecloths -- or preserving them
between leaves of Opera anthologies?

WEATHER FORECAST

Cold makes no sound
a hand is lost

in the snow
traveller's

advisories cloud
the teacups

your heart wrapped
in tinfoil

smokes
like dry ice

caught down the
sink, words

in back of
your throat rise

white against
ruined

sky, then drop
like wind

in a fork of
trees.

THE NIGHT OF TWENTY-SIX BELOW

Our minds grew sluggish, pulses low,
the fire embraced us in its fold;
like wounded wolves, we crawled inside
the farthest corner of the cave:
shared vulnerability to cold.

If we were waked before our time,
denied the cloak that slumber wears,
reluctantly we shook the frost
embedded in ancestral flesh
of hibernating gods and bears.

Presentiment of season, fair --
its name we knew, but could not say,
like perfume daubed behind the ears
or flaming color undefined by
winter's tincture, tainted grey.

Shaggy-furred, we stagger forth,
the spark of life still burning keen,
for our procrastination stirs
a dark desire to test the heave
of swollen rivers, rising green.

THE AMBIGUOUS SNOWBANK

Acting out our misshapen dreams,
a snowbank climbs the sky,
its arrogant poses look familiar --
we shudder, averting our eyes.

Proud as a lion sprawled on all fours,
it holds its pride intact.
Oh, what a shame its sculptured mane
is sullied by alley cats.

A restless white bear, caged in the zoo,
it strikes at the unseen foe,
or like an iceberg furtively glides --
hiding half our secrets below.

At last undone by a merciless sun,
reduced in size it grows;
born to be free but pinioned, like us,
fast to a crumbling floe.

BLOODSAP RISING

After the final snowfall melted,
my backyard was a holy mess -- strewn
with deflated camisoles, Cola cans,
tennis balls. Old twigs, snapped off,
making room; fat buds pointing up, up,
like rude sticky fingers. An insect,
antennae held high, paused: the way
anything doomed may have a sense of it.

The smell of rain and blood. Nearby,
flushed schoolboys pummelled their own.
And the pain of an authentic rainbow
shot a wet arc behind a billboard,
a rooftop; a cloud. Uncoiling, the
wind hissed and stung like an asp. In
defense, the stricken trees ejected
each birth-heavied leafpod headfirst.

SPRING BACCHANALE

Frolicsome trees in frilly green gowns
alluringly pose, and catch the sun's eye.
A tall row of tulips, flaming en masse,
lightens the howls of the amorous cats.

Becalming the wrath of the terrible seas,
kingfishers settle in nautical nests.
Salmon float upstream, tree-sap flows down;
or does it happen, the other way around?

Earth is alive with erogenous zones,
nymphets and satyrs play hide-and-go seek.
But dragon-tailed kites, seduced by a breeze,
flutter in tatters like little boys' hearts.

Defrosting the freezer, I'll thaw my old bones,
hang them to dry on a white picket fence
where typist woodpeckers pick at my brain,
and the air is too thick to finish a sentence

TO THE MOON

Blindman's white eye,
the gossip's left ear,
punctual intruder --
you tread a deadly
path, always
on target.

Now is the time
to break loose,
live by your wits,
take the advice
of an earth maverick:
defy gravity.

Waiting in the wings,
exposed by degrees,

you hang like a
hard, wet snowball
that missed its
mark. Stuck
in a spoke of the
Sorcerer's wheel.

LAST YEAR'S SANDBAR

Something shimmered out there --
a leviathan? a sirene? Lurching
like drunken sailors, we sidestepped
rocks. And shivery-blue, plunged in.

Where the lake floor dropped, we sank
with it. Feet were flippers; arms, fins.
We swam far and easily, muscles powered
by youth. Dangling legs soon struck

the terraced incline. And scaled it.
We emerged, bodies gleaming like brass.
Behind us, the mist-covered shore --
a shrunken line one hand could measure.

Ankle-deep in sediment, we loomed
large as gods, accidentally beached.
The intense glare blinded us. Stumbling,
we laughed and splashed our way back.

DOOR COUNTY THIEF

Dreaming of Eve, I followed
 suit, seduced by the thought
of off-limits fruit.

The apple I sought hung high
 as a kite. Oh, how delicious,
each sinful bite.

The orchard desisting, offered
 resistance: reluctant to
yield to my insistence. Note:

A stem twisted back with care
 and alacrity, assures you and me --
the fruits of posterity!

Since chewing eschewed my
 favorable chances, I clung to
the limbs of wavering branches.

Thrown to my feet, I lost
 my picked prize. The trees only
smiled with wicked, red eyes.

SONG OF THE SEVENTH DECADE

Elatedly I feel young
despite my well-lined face,
watching seedlings sprout,
imbued with petaled grace.

Belatedly I feel free,
a playful, giddy clown,
hearing nighthawks squeal
before they nosedive down.

And lately I feel brave
prepared to take a chance,
spying one lone squirrel
perform its highwire dance.

ADVICE TO A NOVICE GARDENER

When I die, place a cutting of me
in a glass of clear water. Weeks
later, observe a pale-eyed foetus
swimming along the sides. Quickly
unravel its tangle of afterbirth.
Plant it. Watch a shiny green head
puncture the ground, arms jabbing
at the sun. By midsummer, you'll
recognize me -- third plant, right:
clotted with leaves and toughening.

II

Taken From Life

dedicated
to my Mother,
Lottie Robinsky Brown
(1893 - 1989)

*"Show me a woman who does not hide
in the locket of bone that deep eye
beam of fiercely gentle love
she once had from mother,
daughter, sister."*

from THE BOOK OF RUTH AND NAOMI,
by Marge Piercy

BREAK-IN

When death invades, it steals the best away --
Heart, mind, bone; radiant eye.
Shattering the hourglass of day.

Robbed of memory, her mind's a blank,
Melodies stripped bare: the notes, awry.
When death invades, the music steals away.

The life they made, like potters molding clay,
Reft of shape, it cannot satisfy,
Shattering the hourglass of day.

What tragedy may prosody forestay?
Rhyming only draws her tightened sigh
When death invades, it steals the breath away.

Acceptance grows, but never put at bay,
Questions (to the void), the nagging, "Why?"
Shattering the hourglass of day.

His hold at last released, she finds the way
Out of grief. Lost love to crucify.
When death invades, it steals the best away,
Shattering the hourglass of day.

TO KARL WALLENDA

Only circus people know
I wear a jeweled bodysuit
in my fantasies, and a freak
smiles in my hand-mirror.

Climbing the ropespun ladder,
I'd steal a forbidden glance
down, but your ghost-eyes nudge me
like a gun's pointed barrel.

Toes tensed, I strut the highwire
still tingling with your footsteps,
while I juggle six bodies,
your famed "Human Pyramid",

dogged by accident and death.
I pause midway, fists gripping
the balance-pole. Earth rotates
another notch. I think of

San Juan where you plummeted,
unexpectedly, from grace.
The wire was held taut between
two swank oceanside hotels:

a publicity stunt, yet
encountering the tradewinds,
you raged like a fierce storm god --
white-haired Zeus -- caught off-balance.

Like you, I walk the razor's
edge without a net below,
determined as you were, to
give the crowd an honest thrill.

SWEE-TOUCH-NEE TEA

Sold in small tin chests,
it was my grandfather's
solace. He sipped it
boiling hot, in a metal-
lined glass. Sweetened
it with jelly and a sugar
cube pressed to his teeth.
Stirred it slowly with a
silver "tinkling" spoon,
and a long, wheezy sigh.

Born in Lichtenstein,
short, stocky, proud,
he sported a trim goatee
I loved to tug, forcing him
to "growl" like a bear.
The times he visited us,
he carried a wood cane, a
copy of THE FORWARD, and
the stained tobacco smell
of his Sweet Caporals.

I've been to Maxwell St.
where he lived, and my
mother was born. A flat
behind his bakery, next to
the mysterious Gypsies.

The walls were unbleached,
like bread flour. Squat as
a potbellied Lucifer, his
cast-iron stove spat flames
from a wired, grate mouth.

At dawn, its sullen glare
woke him. Bakers' hours.
But if the children still
slept, he reached over
and made quick love to his
second wife, the tall one
who wore gold earrings,
a dark, driven woman we
secretly called, "the crazy"
but never, Grandmother.

MOTHER-IN-LAW

Odors of fish, cabbage soup,
cling to your walls, the lobby
downstairs, and my dreams.
From a bottomless drawer
of keys, string, pins and
empty spools, you select
two Silvercup Bread wrappers.
And present them to me
like a gift from the Czar.

You were eighteen, or fifteen,
when you fled your village
near Minsk. Your uncle forged
your age; your rabbi-father
refused. And so, you sailed
away to the promised land of
Hart, Schaffner & Marx, where
they taught you to sew a seam.

Old warrior, now you sit,
lost in "AS THE WORLD TURNS."
I long to snap off the TV
and say, "Little mother--
in your house I can shout,
get angry; enjoy a 'smoke' with you
on the good couch, without feeling guilty."

Instead, I pretend to read poetry
while plotting my escape.
Your voice coaxes, "Stay a while . . .
What's the rush?" Rising abruptly,
I stuff William Butler Yeats
into one of your bread-bags,
along with my answer.

MORNING EXCURSION

Mechanical as
clockwork, the
palsied figure

defies fate, mind
and space. An empty
cart is the ballast

both hands seize.
But one arm, freed,
aims high as if

hurling a ball, a dare.
Before the sudden
collapse-- limbs

trunk, jerked back;
then the deep lunge
forward. So, cart

and pusher score
another point. A
mankind-sized step

to the moon. To the
corner store. A dumb-
show of advances and

retreats, doorpost
to curb. Primordial
propulsion. Neurons,

synapse, muscular
tic. The switchboard
blazes. A mute voice

shrieks, No! to sick-
bed, to wheelchair.
To any standstill.

WHEN IT RAINS, IT RAINS

It rains, it rains
on her highrise
on eyelids, puffy
as tenth-story clouds
when she looks down
something leaps at her
from the rainforest.

It rains, it rains
on her fists
tight as sonnets
if I open them gently
scanning the lines
will I find the key
to her childhood?

It rains, it rains
on Holiday fish
simmering in a brine
of carrots and onions
on pots stacked away
on a *knipple* she saved
under the kitchen towels.

It rains, it rains
on a snapshot
of her wedding, when
the bride wore black
the color of War-clouds
that shook the world
that grew in our house.

It rains, it rains
on my father, driving
a Packard convertible
his vagabond heart
fanned to flame
though he had left
us, times before.

Cores and rinds
memory scraps, these
she incinerates at
the end of the hall
my mother walks
more slowly when
it rains, it rains.

knipple: (Yiddish) Money saved for a rainy day.

PASSOVER FOR THE RESIDENTS

They were brought downstairs
early. For each: a small
Seder plate of matzos, apple-
sauce, parsley, roasted egg.
Horseradish and fish-balls.

All went well, but someone at
Table Six took a sip of wine
before the first blessing. Was
it Ida, who burst into tears
and begged to leave the room?

Anna was festive in black silk,
faux pearls. Her remaining leg
sported a T-strap sandal...
Later, they sang songs praising
(in unison) God's miracles --

"Day-Day-Enu! Day-Day-Enu!"
Clapping like children; like
Seers whose practiced hands
summon the past. After the
meal, they were wheeled down

a corridor, only to wait at
the Center's stalled elevator.
Suddenly they were Israelites,
"come out of Egypt". Huddled at
the edge of the Red Sea,

praying it would open.

SOLDIERS NOT FOUND ON BATTLEFIELDS

On Sundays, they flock
to the Visitors' Lounge
and sit poised, as birds,
on flamingo couches.
A picture window offers
a blue bowl of sky,
a spoonful of lake.

They nap, or crowd
the TV, awash in "soaps".
No scripts match their own.
Even Mary Ann watches.
Earlier, she screamed
down the hall, and
struck a nurse.

A chatty sparrow
chirps on the patio --
Make the best of it!
Make the best of it!
They draw their shawls
tighter, and smile:
What else can we do?

OF BUGGIES AND WHEELCHAIRS

The halls are swept clean
of nurses, at lunch.
Do not fret, Mother, I'll

attend your ablutions.
Snap-on diapers,
Johnson's talc, baby oil.

You submit without a
murmur. You have little
left to hide. Come

let me lift and dress you,
take you for a stroll.
I'll play young matron,

pushing an English carriage,
showing off the new baby.
Though each time your

wheelchair hits a sidewalk's
crack, my slipped disc
screams. And you moan

from your blankets. A
mummy, wrapped in bandages.
We return from the ramp

and you mutter, "Fix your
belt. It's twisted!"
Mother, I still bristle

at your commands. But
why am I calmer now that
you've grown helpless?

VERSE GAMES

You wake from a nap,
staring at me
as if I were a stranger
whispering your name.

I file your nails;
tweeze eyebrows, and chin.
Lowering your eyes, you
smile like a penitent,

being blessed. You speak
of the residents --
wondering who is Jewish,
and what time is it?

A bedcord is your lifeline.
Once, you were mine.
You recall my birth,
the uncle who called me

a skinny monkey, and chided
you for bearing another
girl. What does it matter
today, in the Lounge --

holding my hand, you ask
why my eyes have grown
smaller. And where are
my poems? We play verse-games:

I begin. "If Winter comes...?"
You answer, "Can Spring
be far behind?" declaiming
the syllables like an

aging orator. My turn:
"The North Wind doth blow.."
Yours: "And we shall have snow."
I try a favorite:

"Good-night, good-night,
parting is such sweet sorrow..."
But today, Juliet's farewell
will be left, unfinished.

Unlocking your chair,
you wheel back to your room.
Wait. Wave me good-bye,
". . . till it be morrow."

GRANDMA'S JET PLANES

Pink contrails streak a summer sky.
The criss-cross lines reminding me
of those she sketched in years gone by --
my children, wide-eyed at her knee.

"Two lines across, two down, you'll find
a place for X; a place for 0".
And if they marked three of a kind,
she added, "Fine. That's tic-tac-toe."

Or trails were string her fingers wound
to make Cat's Cradle. Loop-de-loo!
Delighting tots who early found
what Grandma could, with much ease, do.

Toy jacks were stars she sought to keep,
a rubber ball, the bouncing sun.
She scooped up all in one hand-sweep
before you'd say, "Jack Robinson!"

Pink contrails streak a summer sky.
The criss-cross lines reminding me
of lines she sketched in years gone by,
when Mike was two, and Bonnie, three.

WINTER, 1989

It was the coldest December
on record, but mild
for her funeral, the kind
of day she'd go out
walking, hatless.

I watched her slip below:
the box strewn with flowers,
pallbearers' gloves.
The pulleys sang,
the belts snapped.

Observing these, I saw
nothing. Did she, after
ten decades, regard death
with the same cold eye?

That night the sky clouded,
like a misty window.
Wiping it clear, using
(in her words), "a little
elbow grease," I found
the moon lying on its side.
Like a body at rest.

Two nights later, the moon
reappeared, upright,
full-faced. Or was it
my mother beaming at me --
half-pleased, half-amused
at her fate?

SHIVA

1:33 a.m. When it happened,
a clock spun crazily, marking
the chapel, funeral service,
and gravediggers pouncing,
soundless as cats. Time to
return home and sit *shiva*.

A door swung open, as earth did
for her. Someone grabbed my wrist,
waltzed me down a hall ablaze
with light. Tables of cakes,
fruit, flowers; family solace
intoxicated me like wine.

The music stopped.
The room grew dark as a cave.
Shadows wavered: a thick taper
in a blood-red glass, the
yahrzeit candle, fibrillated
seven days, seven nights.

I watched it melt down to a fiery
wick in a waxen pool. I heard
her voice sputter, go out,
I remembered her lips, how I
cooled them with crushed ice,
I remembered my mother was dead.

NON-INTERVENTION

When she accepted neither food nor drink,
the nurses spoke of stomach tubes. But we
refused to let her linger at the brink --
Arguments ensued until, at last,
they saw our point of view. We asked, "How long
can she survive?" They gave no guarantee.
So we were left to watch and watch her die.
A kind of self-inflicted penalty.

A GRAVE NOURISHMENT

Snowflakes fell today
  obliterating sound,
I thought of one who lay
  restless underground.

Obliterating sound,
  the gasp of empty breath
hidden underground,
  spoon-fed now, by death.

The gasp of empty breath,
  a thirsty mouth below
spoon-fed now, by death,
  quenched by melting snow.

A thirsty mouth below
  sipping while asleep,
quenched by melting snow,
  rootlets, juicy, sweet.

Sipping while asleep,
  berries lined her bed,
rootlets, juicy, sweet,
  easing hunger's dread.

Berries lined her bed,
  I thought of one who lay
easing hunger's dread:
  snowflakes fell today.

UNEXPECTED CALLER

A tap on the door
and Sorrow appears,
its toe wriggles past
your look of surprise.

Suspicions aside,
you play the good host
and, taking its coat,
surrender your chair.

Then, torn by regrets
and sorely depressed,
you pray it will leave --
immediately.

But as the years pass,
you learn to accept
this permanent guest
with faint dignity.

III

A Beating of Wings

SPEAKING TO GOD AT STARVED ROCK

Forgive me,
I am unable to pray.
Spent, speechless
as these canyon walls.

My life, a random
leaf, descends. Will
the pool, darkened
below, retrieve it?

A beating of wings;
a cry, an echo. Craggy
trees lock horns,
vying for sunlight.

Unlike the tiny fern
whose green fist
clamps shut, I open
at Your touch.

CONSPIRACY

Midnight, late fall. I'm still awake,
not in bed but chilled on the porch,
waiting for a few friends to share
the time. For example, the renowned

Dipper I earlier saw, north/northwest,
behind the yard's sloping garage.
Where did the moon go, after its face
was fully unmasked? Vanished like

Venus, the planet I need to steady
my course. From this perch, the sky
resembles a vast room where, I swear,
something was whisked, dragged away,

seconds ago. A sea of tranquility but
contrived, shot through with holes.
Among the missing I count: Dog Star,
Hunter, Queen In Her Glittering Chair.

Dawn stars are more arrogant, with
the sky to themselves. Like perfect
strangers, they stand together, cold-
eyed distant, laughing at my losses.

EMIGRE

You, the alien angel,
awaken to thunderbolts
of alarm, warmed-over
maelstrom for breakfast.
A mirror, its vacant eye
of daylight, confirms
your wound. Stuffing
your tattered plumage
in a frogman's wet suit,
you flop through streets
of gravely swelling ocean.

MEMORIES OF VIETNAM

Oh, to be a soldier stationed
in the CuChi foothills, I'd get
to see the Bob Hope Christmas Show,
join the G.I. laughter, feel my
manhood swelling at the sight of
the All-American bosom, bouncing
in a patriotic frenzy, while I'd
clap my hands, and stamp both feet
(unless one was missing), and bawl
out loud to "Silent Night", until
the last musician shut his case,
and Bob Hope's starlets danced
into the sky like specks of flak,
and I'd go back to killing without
time to ask: what was I laughing at?

SLAUGHTERHOUSE GOAT

With biblical
head, face deadpan,
thick upper lip
raised (a sob? a
sneer?), he is the
coy accomplice
who uses a
ploy of bells -- the
clang, seductive
around his neck --
and knows how to
step back with great
delicacy
moments before
the ready rush
of sheep up the
ramp and through a
Walpurgisnacht
that jerks them up
by one lamb's leg
each, and two bleats
of complaint. Then
the billy goat,
dismissed by his
trainer in stiff
uniform and
electric prod,
retires to the
yard, nuzzling bits
of crushed gravel --
innocent as
any Judas.

THE KILLING FLOOR

Remember the ancients
who were buried in their
bridal finery? Here,
the dressed cattle are wound
in sheets, and ushered out.
The severed heads, massive
as Minotaurs minus
their ungodly bodies,
dangle eyeless, on hooks.
Think of John the Baptist --
lust's decapitation.

Remember the woman
who made love to his head
on a silver charger?
She snake-danced around it,
like men in red aprons
slitting the hides with wild
two-step, guttural cries.
Above the fray, as if
by instinct,each carcass
waits its turn to be hosed,
wiped clean of memory.

LAPSE

Why do I think of famine
in times of plenty -- or
imagine your body will vanish,
leaving no imprint on mine?

Why do I conjure up spectres
of those who sleep alone
in shade-darkened rooms?
Look, I am the world's coward,
taught to fear loneliness;
they are the brave.

Yet as I watch you,
your face mapped by sleep,
a sea change transforms me --

I am the crescent moon,
squinting one eye
at the landscape below.
Hills, bridges, turrets,
grown more beloved. Tonight,
at the turn of my dark cycle.

MEDICAL POEM

I scalpel your X-rayted
brain scan above my
allergy-prone bed.

A massive migraine
erupted after our last
conjugal fracture.

My left ventricle flaps
on the clothesline with
your cancerous wool socks.

You will never know
the pain of an arterio-
sclerotic heart. Or

find the pressure points
of a purple rose that
can't stop hemorrhaging.

DRIVER'S TEST

While driving east
to Foster Beach,
I saw a man
remove his briefs
and frolic in
the summer storm.

His skin was wet
and deeply tanned,
except the place
his member lay,
unperturbed by
motorists' scorn.

He hailed a friend
in birthday suit
and like two gods,
Hermes and Zeus?
they danced away
past honking horn.

While driving east
to Foster Beach,
I gripped the wheel
and saw revealed
intriguing form
of pretense, shorn.

TRIO

Let the soul
dance, leap
to your side.

Like a masked
partner, it will
elevate you

and guide
your feathery
descent.

Then, with a
flick of
its wrist

(the circle
of spotlight
narrowing),

it turns
and pivots
the other. The

one still
poised, wing-
less as you.

DANCING IN THE DARK

Tonight the band blares, "Celebration!"
then stops, and plays
a set of Golden Oldies.
All the aging couples rise
as one, drawn to the Maestro's baton
like children, to the Piper's tune.
He stands aside, a shadowy Timekeeper,
putting us through our paces,
"Ah-l, Ah-2, Ah-1-2-3-4!"

When we were young, we danced everywhere --
weddings, ballrooms, the Chez Paree.
Or we danced at home, while
Kate Smith sang, "Shine On, Harvest Moon!"
her voice amplifying the radio,
God and America. Later, exhausted,
we fell asleep on Kate's bosom,
full-fleshed as the moon.

In World War II you danced
in a Texas bar if your boot-camp
was lucky and got a weekend pass.
At Normandy, you danced ashore,
dodging artillery. Back home,
I went solo to the local USO.

But tonight, we dance together.
And though your expression is remote
as the Man in the Moon's, there's
electricity in your arms. I dangle,
like Gepetto's Pinocchio, obeying
every dip, every curve of your body.
For this strange blue dress I am wearing
has a wicked flounce that unlocks
my resistance. Yes tonight, we hear

strains of Sammy Kaye, Kay Kyser,
Count Basie and the Duke. Tonight,
we will show our children, our
moon-begotten children, our rhythm
& blues, rock & roll children --
("Ah-l, Ah-2, Ah-1-2-3-4!")

how we danced.

DRIVING WEST OF THE LAKE

Midsummer heat.
I lower one window
halfway; tune the car radio.
Charlie "Bird" Parker,
his saxophone soars
on satin wings.

I pass hawkers, gawkers.
Hookers. And pushers,
macho in lO-gallon hats,
dispensing favors
in small brown bags.

Men, diminutive as
Mayan warriors, wait idly
in doorways. Tomorrow,
they will make
their own history.

Women on stone steps
suckle babies.
The muffled cries of
the loneliest foghorn;
the last B-train
heading home. A siren's
crescendo, heads nowhere.

I unplug
a Diet Coke, it hisses
at me. Head tilted back--
steady now-- I drink
the Big City down. All
the forgotten,
unMagnificent Miles.

The announcer signs off:
"Take it easy, but take it."

I drive on.

THE EXILES

Remember the seven
women who fasted
for ERA's passage?
One, a robust ex-
Mormon, thought the
fast was manageable.
Unlike the thinnest,
Sonia, who lost one
or two pounds a day.

Yes, the same Sonia
Johnson, renounced
by the Church, and
her "soul-searching"
husband. Wasted and
unable to walk, she
sat in a wheelchair,
pushed by the others
to Capital chambers.

Or they stood alone
on a patch of State
ground, historically
reserved for witches.
Did they hunger for
the old ways? Miss
the taste of social
acceptance? Homilies
once nourished them.

On TV, they gave us
few clues. Faceless,
appearing to blanch
like certain plants
exposed to sunlight,
they kept vigil. Or
eyes shut, dreamt of
votes, and the smell
of bacon, sizzling.

LONG DISTANCE

I

I hold your young life
in my right hand,
the way I once cradled it.
Now the giver receives
your sounds, welcome as
apples falling in air.

I measure my words, as if
I were shucking peas,
looking for the greenest.
Or I speak too rapidly,
afraid the operator might
sever our connection.

II

"Hello, Mom. I'm feeling fine!"
you rang me twice today.
Shall I guess the unexpressed
behind the words you say?

Options, risks, brave new paths,
I tip my hat to you--
explorer of exotic shores.
In my day, I had few.

Yours, a world of lasers, chips,
computers, future shock.
And the ticking, day and night --
biological clock.

And Mothers, kept in dark?
My dear, it happens all the time.
In my youth, I must admit,
I hid the truth from mine.

A POEM IN FIVE ACTS AT STRATFORD

Thin walls, thin towels, traffic noise.
Here we'd stay for the great Bard's plays.
On the dresser, we found a comb
and silver brush, and felt like children
often warned, "Do Not Touch!"

After "The Tempest", we hurried back
like Florentine lovers to their tryst.
Only the landlady slept next door --
deaf, adrift in her midsummer's dream,
but we froze in bed, afraid she'd hear us.

Seated downstairs, facing the fire
or a "Winter's Tale" oracle,
Thomas, her son, mused about life:
why had his father died of bad teeth
while extracting a filial oath?

Faithful as Lear's youngest child,
Tom kept the widow entertained --
dined her at Kitchener, Blyth or Guelph.
Her eyelids heavied with wine; bodice
heaving, laced with maternal guilt.

Mornings, she ate our leftover scones;
then cooed at the parakeet Tom had bought
after the last one tried to escape,
and struck the wall. A crushed, blue rose.
Outside, a truck rattled our cage.

SOUVENIR

She views the filmy past
in album pages, frayed.
Her veil of bridal lace,
his arm around her waist.
Evanescence, stayed.

A painted carousel.
Saddled loose, they ride
with escalating grace
above, below the ring,
past each wary face.

Picnic, sunlight. Shade.
They linger motionless,
then draw apart. Their pose
predicts the outcome well.
A final frame. Farewell.

Despite the copyist's trade,
occasion bittersweet
its duplicate, resists.
Love, once held, alone
in memory exists.

LITTLE THEATRE ON HOWARD STREET

When sunset's backdrop falls
and night upstages day
    kaleidoscopic signs
    erupt like stars ablaze
their glare illuminates
the street of no return.

Undaunted by the past
new storefronts bravely rise
    as late October rains
    expunge the air of sin
and life transformed by art
opens at Wisdom Bridge.

In Brian Friel's play
a Healer of the faith
    condemned to ply his trade
    to Celtic countryfolk
is nightly crucified
by those incurables.

The sickly and the weak
(a charlatan's delight!)
    defrauded by his touch
    escape with ghostly steps
across the narrow heights
the depths of Howard Street.

And yet in crowded rooms
above the juke-box bars
    men dressed in undershirts
    unlock their steel guitars
while overlooking grief
they strum a salsa beat.

Their voices drift along
the corner fiddle shop
    where instruments in view
    are carved and rubbed by hand
bare wood once virginal
conceivable of song.

HIGH HOLIDAY SERVICE

The old man
in his new suit
sat straight as a
taper listening to
each word of the
sermon when

suddenly his
hearing-aid sang
out, at first in a
squeaky voice then
spiraling above
the pulpit

it became
unnerving like
the long smothered
cry of some dybbuk
that shocked the
congregation

pretending
not to notice
until at last the
man with slightly
tremulous hands
unscrewed it

and sighing
dropped it into
a hip pocket, the
place he kept all
his unanswered
prayers.

REVISING HISTORY

Wake up, friend,
it's just a hoax --
you never died
at Auschwitz.

Come, relax,
have some tea:
pick your teeth,
the gold-filled ones.

What makes stripes
on your coat?
The moon in flight
behind the trees.

Yellow star
upon your chest?
It fell to earth,
Heaven's gift.

And that stench
of burning flesh?
A *dybbuk* hides
in chimney smoke.

All is well,
rest in peace;
you never died
at Auschwitz.

SCIATICA

It stung my leg like a
sniper's bullet. Frantic,
I limped to Dr. Soong,
saw him unroll an ancient
stargazer's chart. On it,
the Seven Pleiades were
acupuncture points linking
stars to the nerve center
of the universe. And the back
of my right leg. Pain has a
high and low, yin and yang
flow. I only felt its hardset
jaw. After my treatment, the
doctor said little. He locked
his pride in an ivory box
with his thousand-year old
needles. Then sat on the floor
in lotus position. And read
the Wall Street Journal.

REFLECTIONS

Awakened by rain,
I lazily watch
foot-puddles erupt,
collapse, and leap back
with each direct hit.

The shimmering streets
evoke memories
of sunlit oak floors,
preserved artifacts,
a Vermont museum.

Someone had placed, so
casual it seemed,
a stereoscope
and box of old slides,
on a wicker chair.

Inserting each frame,
I entered the lives,
the faded affairs
of Brattleboro's
Drum & Bugle Corps.

Survivors of war,
of North against South,
they sat in three rows;
their uniforms, creased,
irrevocably.

Attempting to speak,
they stared at my face
or some point beyond,
the terror they felt
could not be described.

But I drew them close
and heard whispers low
of blood-spattered fields,
of brothers who fell,
the drummer-boys' roll.

SURVIVOR

The last hydrangea
I forgot to pick
hangs outside
my kitchen window.

Capped with a
snowy yarmulke,
its shorn head
trembles

whenever I light
two Sabbath candles,
and only one
wick catches.

TO WHITEY, LOVING CAT

Death and cremation
no wintry grave -- strewn ashes
spawn pussy willows

OPERATING PROCEDURE

We are wakened at dawn
and taxied down the
hospital corridor.

Only to wait our turn like
airplanes, lined up
in a holding pattern.

Nurses, chattering nearby,
stop to see if our seat-
belts are fastened.

Feeling light-headed, I am
reconciled to the rest
of the journey.

Motors revved, our cots
spring forward. Is this
adrenalin propulsion?

The surgeon has the blank
look of a pilot
entering the cockpit.

He pulls on his gloves.
"Arrivals and Departures"
a well-kept secret.

JEU D'OEIL

The lone runner
binds me to his eye.
I hold him
in the chambers
of mine, allowing
enough slack
for his widening
arc. If I turn aside,

he moves among
the tall grasses
of my retina.
If I look ahead,
he drops into
its blind hole.

THE MERMAID'S VERSION

A silver-haired jogger
runs along the beach.
Once, he found me

adrift. Wiping my
blue sand, he pleased,
he terrified me. And

I forgot the sea.
Now he races, arms,
akimbo, mouth pursed

to a slit, like a
fish caught on a hook.
Legs thrash air,

head with bloody eye
rears towards sky,
sinks fast. My turn

to bring the jogger
ashore. Holding his body
tightly as treasure,

I hear a cry. I hear
my life, cresting like
a wave, within him.

METRA STATION

I saw them across the tracks,
commuters, waiting for the 5:38.
I glanced away, then back.
The platform was emptied.
Men, women, children. Train.
Vanished, gone.

A torn billboard sign
with scrawled graffiti,
mocked my disbelief.

They took the details with them:
paisley scarf, rag doll,
leather brief case. If only
they had looked at me -- or
I had held them longer --
sparks flown across the gulf.

How could I retrieve
a band of anonymous commuters
from oblivion? I thought of
Orpheus searching Hades
for the beloved. Disobeying
the gods, he looked back
at Eurydice too soon,
and lost her, forever.

The myth chills me.
Or was it a raw wind, blowing
from the city? Down the tracks,
a blurred shape silently
rounded the bend.

COMMUTER COMPANION

He begs me for change,
enough for his ride.
The evils of booze
have cost him his pride.

A cross-country drifter,
boxcars he'd grab,
and once rode first-class
in the engineer's cab.

Obsessively clean,
thinks vermin a bore;
takes baths in Times Square
near Salvation's Store.

He's known many women,
he once had a wife
(Lady Fear sleeps with him
most of his life).

A few flophouse pals,
relationships, strained.
His hands keep shaking,
nicotine stained.

And so he rambles
while clouds threaten rain
and we stand waiting
for the Northwestern Train.

It comes round the bend--
its front light blinking
like his right eye,
bloodshot, from drinking.

Sit with me? he asks,
my gaze travels far.
And that's when he caught
the last "SMOKING" car.

GRANT PARK REMEMBERED

August, 1988, the long drought
ends, the Jazzmen are back.
We flock across tightly drawn

lines and sit, ten thousand
as one -- a family, cheering its
legends: Ammons, Gillespie,

Ellington. August, 1968, we
were here, listening to the
jazzy beat of the mounted

police, soft-shoe shuffle,
advance, retreat. The obscene
Convention, undeclared War,

false bodycount; long-haired
troubadours sang protest songs
to tone deaf politicans. A

minicam toppled, the screen
banked like a jet when the
sky reels and Lake Michigan

falls in your lap. A shatter of
glass, truncheon's raw smack:
whose son waved from the back

of a paddy wagon? Did Garibaldi's
steel steed charge the besieged
Hilton? In the Park? Then,

not now. No bloodied headbands
tonight, only a face-off
between tenor sax men. Their

music clears the lake breeze
of yesterday's tear gas; the
queasy smell of tomorrow.

We cheer and dance in the
aisles, crowded with ghosts of
Yippies, Weathermen, martyrs

and clowns -- long denied a
park permit. We lean towards the
truth of Joe Williams' blues,

Sonny Rollins' riffs. In raucous
jam session, the Jazzmen rouse
the City sleeping beyond

the rose garden, fountain flaming,
painted harbor boats, the out-
law wildflowers. And we sit

listening to sweet hot jazz,
unlike twenty years ago. Here
on this grassy knoll. Yes, here.

FLYING HOME ON A DC-7

As I glance down from thirty thousand feet
Securely fastened in my window seat,
I sight a strange plateau on which I find
The marked configurations of my mind:
Cranial grooves where indecisions lie
Unresolved, my ghosts afraid to die,
Submerged cathedrals of a wasteland soul
(My middle ear records for whom they toll),
"And to the right. . ." a shape of near recall,
Yet overcast with recollection's pall.
And desiccated lunar valley streams
Where I moonwalk, weightless in my dreams.

Like Alice peering through a keyholed door,
I find impressed upon the ceiling floor
My infant steps, the early childhood scars
That hang in place like night's emerging stars,
Like prints on snow the polar sled-dogs make
Or sandbar tracks beneath a crystal lake.
Perhaps, the path of prehistoric man
Long fossilized before this trip began.
Cast ashore, and later standing tall,
He carved the horned bison on the wall
Till words emerged in his unpatterned deep,
Awaking frozen hemispheres of sleep.

The vision passes. Mists obscure my view.
"Prepare to land. . ." And enter life, anew?
How effortless, and yet quite turbulent,
This pressurized inferno of descent!
I sense the drop of wheels like birthing pain
(Am I the foetus of a womb-shaped plane?),
And see my life below in bold relief,
A crowded, convoluted cloverleaf,
A traffic grid of fleur-de-lys entwined
With catatonic limbs, in chrome, confined.
I exit, leaving on some cloudy shelf --
The rising moon, the North Star, and myself.

Epilogue
FIRST OFFERINGS

These few have survived, apart from the rest,
Prepared to sing on their own.
Faces, well-scrubbed; voices, on-key;
The offspring I have sown.

And yet, and yet -- the others, stillborn --
I feel a sense of loss:
When I aborted their unfinished songs,
Did I shed myself with the dross?

About the Author

Gertrude Rubin's poetry springs from her Chicago roots. She studied at Northeastern Illinois University on the northwest side; received her MFA degree from the Writers' Program, University of Illinois at Chicago, 1978. She is a four-time "Dial-A-Poem, Chicago!" reader.

Her work has been published in anthologies, including the Anthology of Magazine Verse, 1985. She won Grand Prize (away from home!) in the Indiana State Poetry Contest, 1986.

She is active in the Poets Club of Chicago; and helped organize group readings at Guild, Rizzoli's Bookstore, the Chicago Public Library Cultural Center. And, in Evanston, at the Chicago Historical Bookworks.

Gertrude has performed her own readings at Skokie Library, the Apocolypse Literary Series, and various Chicago coffee-houses. She did a two year stint of readings at local nursing homes and senior citizen centers. And for five years, served as program convenor for disabled adults at the Mayer Kaplan Community Center.

She is also author of THE PASSOVER POEMS, published in January, 1991, by Evanston Publishing, Inc., Evanston, IL 60202. Gertrude lives in Chicago with her husband and trusty typewriter.

Acknowledgements

Grateful acknowledgement is given to the publications in which these poems (some, revised) first appeared:

Descant, Overtures, Rhino, Willow Review, Salome, Mati, Dark Horse, Cresset, Kaleidoscope, Impressions, Anthology of American Verse (1985), American Anthology of Midwestern Poetry (1987), Naming the Daytime Moon, Romancing the Past, Feminist Writers Literary Supplement, Jewish Currents, Jewish Frontier, and Sound & Light.

Also, "Dial-A-Poem, Chicago!"; Indiana State Poetry Contest (won Grand Prize, 1986); Beloved of the Muse Contest, Poetry Haven (tied for first place, 1972), and the book THE PASSOVER POEMS, Evanston Publishing, Inc. January, 1991.

About the Author's Work

As a writer of narrative poems that are poignant and life-affirming, Gertrude Rubin ranks with the best of modern poets.

Rebecca Moskowitz
Wilmette Freelance Writer, Teacher MONNACEP (Maine, Oakton, Northfield, Niles Adult Continuing Education)

A BEATING OF WINGS is one of those delightful volumes of poetry that give the reader the opportunity of meeting a lovely human being. "Let the soul dance," writes Gertrude Rubin. My soul indeed danced with hers so many times. *Soul* is the key word here -- the part that lasts.

> *When I die, place a cutting of me*
> *in a glass of clear water.*

No need. These poems are her soul sprouting already.

Allan Bates
English Department., Northeastern University, Chicago, Illinois

Sensitive to life's rhythms, to the natural world and the curious realm of human feeling and connections, these poems face life and death with wide-open eyes. Never flinching, they show what is and push beyond the surface to strength and grace.

Jill Baumgaertner
Associate Professor of English, Wheaton College.